animal babies

in rainforests

KINGFISHER

Kingfisher Publications Plc
New Penderel House
283–288 High Holborn
London WC1V 7HZ
www.kingfisherpub.com

First published by Kingfisher Publications Plc 2004

10 9 8 7 6 5 4 3 2 1

1TR/0104/TWP/PICA(PICA)/150STORA

Copyright © Kingfisher Publications Plc 2004

A CIP catalogue record for this book is available from the British Library.

0 7534 0942 9

Author and Editor: Jennifer Schofield
Designer: Joanne Brown
Jacket design: Joanne Brown
Picture manager: Cee Weston-Baker
Picture researcher: Rachael Swann
DTP manager: Nicky Studdart
DTP co-ordinator: Sarah Pfitzner
Senior production controller: Deborah Otter

Printed in Singapore

animal babies

in rainforests

My golden coat is covered in spots – it looks as if I have flowers all over my back.

Who is my mummy?

My mummy is a jaguar and I am her cub.

My mummy licks me with her bright pink tongue to keep me clean.

When there is danger,
I stand up tall, beat
my chest and make
a very loud noise.

Who is my mummy?

My mummy is a gorilla and I am her baby.

We are such lazy apes that we like to sleep for most of the day.

My nose is a short trunk. I use it like a snorkel when I am in deep water.

Who is my mummy?

My mummy
is a tapir and
I am her calf.

My baby fur is
stripy, but the
stripes will fade
as I grow older.

I like to stare, and the first things you will see are my beady eyes and their black patches.

Who is my mummy?

My mummy is a lemur and I am her baby.

When we are out and about and my little legs grow tired, my mum carries me on her back.

My arms are nearly twice as long as my legs. They make it easy for me to swing through the trees.

Who is my mummy?

My mummy is an orang-utan and I am her baby.

When I am scared, I hold on to my mum so that I do not fall.

I have three sharp claws on my hands and feet. They help me to hang upside down on branches.

Who is my mummy?

My mummy is a sloth and I am her baby.

We are very slow and never hurry to go from here to there.

I have sticky pads under my feet. They help me to sit on the branches of leafy trees.

Who is my mummy?

My mummy is a tarsier and I am her baby.

We can turn our small heads right around, so I am never out of my mum's sight.

Additional Information

Although rainforests cover a very small area of the world – about 7 percent – an extraordinary variety of animals can be found there. They range from biting insects, poisonous frogs and snakes, to butterflies as big as birds, exotic parrots and large apes. The animals in this book are found in various rainforests throughout the world, jaguars, tapirs, and sloths are found in the large rainforests of Central and South America, gorillas live in the African rainforest, lemurs can be found in North East Madagascar, orang-utans in South East Asia, and tarsiers in the rainforests of Indonesia.

Acknowledgements

The publisher would like to thank the following for permission to reproduce their material. Every care has been taken to trace copyright holders. However, if there have been unintentional omissions or failure to trace copyright holders, we apologise and will, if informed, endeavour to make corrections in any future edition.

Cover: Manoj Shah/Getty; Half title Masahiro Iijima/Ardea; Title page: Art Wolfe/Getty; Jaguar 1: Nick Gordon/Ardea; Jaguar 2: Nick Gordon/Ardea; Gorilla 1: Art Wolfe Getty; Gorilla 2 Art Wolfe/Getty; Tapir 1: Tom Brakefield/Corbis; Tapir 2: Slyvain Cordier/Ardea; Lemur 1: Adrian Warren/Ardea; Lemur 2: Adrian Warren/Ardea; Orang-utan 1: Manoj Shah/Getty; Orang-utan 2: Slyvain Cordier/Ardea; Sloth 1: Jany Sauvanet/NHPA; Sloth 2: Kevin Schafer/Corbis; Tarsier 1: Masahiro Iijima/Ardea; Tarsier 2: Patricia and Michael Fogden